"Age is but a number. So, I rebelled."

Timeless Rebel

Empowered to Pursue the Dreams Within

By Dawn Angela Mickens

Copyright © 2014 Dawn Angela Mickens. All rights reserved.

No part of this book may be reproduced without the expressed, written permission of the author.

ISBN-978-1-1-938563-15-7

Published by Literacy Moguls Publishing Co.

PO BOX 2764 SMYRNA, GA 30081
www.literacymoguls.com

Front Cover Image: Jamie Thomson, 702 Photo Studio ; Front Suit Designer: Gayla Rogers, Gayla Rogers Collection; Hair Stylist: Crystal Leisner; Make-up Artist: Kiera Wright; Back Cover Image: John Washington Jr., JWJ Photography

DISCLAIMER

I have tried to recreate events, locales and conversations from my memories of them. In order to maintain their anonymity in some instances I have changed the names of individuals and places, I may have changed some identifying characteristics and details such as physical properties, occupations and places of residence. Although the author and publisher have made every effort to ensure that the information in this book was correct at press time, the author and publisher do not assume and hereby disclaim any liability to any party for any loss, damage, or disruption caused by errors or omissions, whether such errors or omissions result from negligence, accident, or any other cause.

PRAISES for Dawn Angela's Accomplished Journey

"I am so very proud to be your sister and to have been able to watch you persevere in following your dreams despite adversity. I remember so well a conversation we had when you were unexpectedly laid off in your previous career. I had shared that everything happens for a reason and that God was in control. I knew then that you had so much to offer and there was a star for you to reach in the future. You are on that path and I know there is no limit to what you can accomplish in your life. Mom and Dad taught us well and it brings tears to my eyes to see those well-taught lessons through you of "always have a dream and to never give up" on your goals and what you believe in. I look forward to supporting you in any way that I can. I love you Dawn!!!"

—Rachaelle Lynne Richardson, Sister

***

"Like most devoted wives and mothers, Dawn Angela lost herself in the needs of others. Luckily she overcame all obstacles and found herself. Now we all get to benefit from her example of beauty, grace, and perseverance. I'm blessed to know her."

-Gayla Rogers, fashion designer, mother of five

***

"What can I say about DawnAngela? She is a woman with a good spirit and has a heart for those around her. True leader no matter what she's involved in. Seems to know when you need to hear a word. She steps in when you need her; I would trust her with my projects. To me Barbie Doll is bigger than life. Wish the best for you."

-Vanessa Henderson (affectionately Momma V), fashion designer, The House of Van Miller

***

"DawnAngela is the epitome of poise. She embodies many of the critical elements that we wish to see in more women and girls on their quest to love the reflection in the mirror. She owns her age and the room!"

-Ardre Orie, Author of Consciously Beautiful: I Am Enough

***

"Knowing DawnAngela has been a blessing, she is such an inspiration to all women young and old! She's straightforward, honest, encouraging, & non-judgmental. And she doesn't mind sharing her beauty secrets!!! I love her so much!!"

-Katrina Walker (affectionately Sissy)—friend, model, mother of four

***

"...DawnAngela's journey in this life has taken her where she is supposed to be, with her faith and works she will succeed and be wonderfully successful. Age is truly nothing but a number, you are as young as you feel, and as rich as you believe! LIVE, LOVE PROSPER"

-Ms. Nickee Mack—agent & runway coach, Diva Day International, Inc

Dedicated to

My daughter Jenae Ann who inspired me;

My daughter Jaeda Lee who encouraged me;

My son Dj who challenged me;

My husband Darryl Lee who showed patience and guidance;

My mother Dorothy Ann Richardson who provided faith & wisdom; and to

My beloved father, the late Rev. Robert Lee Richardson, who simply loved me for ME.

***

"If I didn't define myself for myself, I would be crunched into other people's fantasies for me and eaten alive."

~Audre Lorde

CONTENTS

Introduction   1

Chapter 1 Shaky Ground: EMPOWERED   6

Chapter 2 Extra-Extra: KEEP IT MOVIN'   17

Chapter 3 Zumba: INSPIRED   36

Chapter 4 A Thin Line: BALANCE   44

Chapter 5 Road Map: DEVELOPMENT   52

Chapter 6 The Make-Over: TRANSFORMATION   68

Chapter 7 The Catwalk: PURPOSE   80

Chapter 8 Model Life: ENCOURAGE   89

Chapter 9 Giving Back: VOLUNTEERISM   105

Chapter 10 Age is but a Number: MOTIVATION   114

Conclusion   123

Dawn Angela's Poems   130

My Model Resume   133

My Acting Resume   135

Acknowledgements   140

INTRODUCTION

At age 46, I have reinvented myself, revamped my career, and rejuvenated my life! I'm living my dreams and enjoying every minute of it! Exactly what does that mean? Well, for me, it means that life didn't stop when I entered into my 40s. Hopefully for you, it will also mean that life doesn't have to stop once you enter into your 40s. It's not doomsday! After all, 40 is the new 20, isn't it? Women are no longer rushing into marriage immediately following high school or college. There is this new urgency for women to secure independence, establish a career and be financially stable before entering into marriage or even having children. Women are now birthing children much later in life; late 30s or even early 40s.

Actresses, Halle Berry, Kim Basinger, Susan Sarandon, and Brooke Shields all birthed their first child while in their 40s. Also, there are plenty of women who have decided to either go back to school, go on road trips with friends or even trying the unconventional way of online dating. I believe that as younger women our attention is directed to what others want; however as we grow into our 40s, we wonder what it is that we want for ourselves. Nowadays it's also typical for women of a more mature age to spring into action and really begin to connect with their inner being in the later years.

There was a point in time when I felt stuck in my life. Especially when devastating events occurred (truthfully a broken nail could be major fallout in my household). But seriously, our daily routines of life in general can take over and before you know it one day, you wake up asking questions such as, "who am I?", "where am I?", or even "what am I?" If we allow it, things can easily spiral out of control. If you've ever questioned your self-worth, your personal identity, or felt stuck in your life then this book is for you! I will take you through my personal journey from finding myself unemployed with very little direction as to what would come next, to becoming a self-made woman and a model in the fashion and entertainment industry.

Oddly enough, the realization of this book began with an encounter with Bishop T.D. Jakes (minister, evangelist, life coach, and speaker). I will share little "take aways" throughout the book of the inspiration and wisdom shared by Bishop Jakes via his T.V. show, "T.D. Jakes Presents: Mind, Body and Soul," and how his words inspired me to go on when I needed them most. But first I must give you some insight as to how that came to fruition.

In February 2011, I unexpectedly found myself unemployed after 20 years in the real estate industry. Just prior to that time I was a supervisor of a real estate title company within a well-established law firm in Atlanta, Georgia. The economy was beginning to tank and layoffs were happening left and right; quicker than any of us could've imagined. Although initially I was upset about losing my job, I was also somewhat relieved. I mean no one wants to be laid off, fired, or kicked to the curb do they? But seriously, I secretly thought to myself, how long could I have pretended to be doing work when there was really nothing to be done?

Frankly, I was feeling burnt out from the entire real estate industry thing anyway, but I also knew I couldn't just sit back and do nothing with my life. So after a little R&R I began the process of submitting resume after resume to no avail. Sure, there were a few interviews and a few close calls;

but nothing with any permanent potential. I found myself overwhelmed with all the new job search engines. Social media and technology in general, with all of its associated lingo gave me a headache. My being frustrated with it all was an understatement. I worked various part-time jobs; however, by this time, I was completely over the traditional 9-to-5 working process. In short, I was miserable.

In August of 2012, a year and a half later, still unemployed, I decided to submit to an ad searching for people who had suddenly found themselves jobless. I made a video clip of myself and submitted it to what turned out to be BETs T.V. show, "T.D. Jakes Presents: Mind, Body and Soul". I thought making the video would be fun and that perhaps I'd be on the show at some point; however as I began my recording, it dawned on me, that I truly felt unimportant, useless, and unworthy. It felt as if I wasn't carrying my weight as a wife and mother. This turned out to be a life changing experience for me. I remember running upstairs and then staring at myself in the mirror while asking myself, "who am I?" To my surprise, I really didn't know the answer.

This is not a "How to Book" on becoming a model or a format of what you should or should not do in life. The goal for readers is to think outside the box. To think of yourself in a totally different way that may propel you to leading a more fulfilled life. "Timeless Rebel: Empowered to Pursue the Dreams Within" is based on some of the highlights of my personal journey. It can also be a blueprint for a personal journey of your own; an inspiration that will empower and enable you to grab hold of your life and run with it!

It's my sole desire to:

- Empower

- Motivate

- Encourage

- Inspire

CHAPTER 1

Shaky Ground: EMPOWERED

*"**Empower**- to give power to someone"*

It was 2011. At a glance, my life at the gracious age of 43 appeared fine. My marriage of 25 years (yes, I said 25 years) was unwavering. My kids, at the time 14, 20 & 21 years old were all growing into their own selves. I felt a level of success with all my accomplishments in the real estate industry and my health was impeccable. Yet it was also in 2011 when everything went wrong. Nothing was lining up with the way I'd envisioned it at the end of 2010.

Suddenly unemployed and bored to tears; I attempted to cure my angst by getting involved with a network marketing company. Ardyss International, specializing in reshaping garments, nutritional, & personal care products known as the home of the "Body Magic". "Body Magic" was our top selling body shaping product and I managed to profit from the sales. However, my time with Ardyss quickly came to an end. Your success in network marketing is largely dependent upon others in your circle to do their part. Well, I was on a quest for independence and didn't have time to wait on others to fulfill their obligations so I made a choice, that network marketing would not be my future. The question was what was going to be next?

    Is this my life? I've never been in a position where I didn't know what I was going to do when I jumped out of bed in the morning. Well, let me rephrase that, I did know that I'd wake my son up and get him out to school. I knew I'd see my husband off to work and I knew I'd feed and let the dog outside. I also knew I'd prepare myself a cup of coffee or tea or "special juice" (don't ask). What I didn't know is what on earth I was going to do with my time while everyone else was off busy with their own lives. Once I realized what I didn't want out of my life, I had to figure out what I did want. A child can reflexively say "no" when they know something doesn't feel good to them but only a fully evolved being can figure out what to say "yes" to and then map out a way to get there. Luckily for me, it was summertime-the best time of the year to take a trip and get away from the mind numbing day to day routine. Sometimes a trip is just an escape for recreation but there are other times when it is part of a journey. This was definitely one of those times. I had to get away from home to find what was lost in me-because my vision of where I could see myself going was painfully out of focus.

My birthday was approaching and my husband and I planned a trip with our son to go to Savannah, Georgia.

"What's in Savannah?" my son asked.

"Well Dj, I answered, Savannah has a lot of cultural history, museums, beaches, and good ole' Southern charm". As a typical teenaged boy, he was just not feeling it. If it wasn't Florida, Cancun or the Virgin Islands…, let's just say, he was not thrilled about the trip.

Little did he know that, a few months back I spent the weekend in Savannah with my girlfriends. That was the first time in a long time that I'd taken a trip without my family in tow. I remember it like it was yesterday. We rented a condo for the weekend and when we arrived we couldn't miss the place. It was the only house with a bright red door and a gold plated door knob. This place was "sexy"! Three levels of party! We ran throughout the house bumping into each other with excitement. The oversized rooms, enormous kitchen, and dual balconies made us feel like queens. And we were within walking distance of everything. The highlight of the trip was our day at Tybee Island Beach, which was very serene. I put my chair on the perfect spot in the sand. Put on the sunglasses. Laid back, turned on Pandora and I finally had a chance to relax my mind. I had been doing way too much thinking up to that point. We had so much fun shopping, touring, eating, sipping and just enjoying each other's company that I thought it'd be a great trip for the family as well. Looking back, I think the reason I wanted to get back to Savannah was not so much that it would be a great trip for "us" as a family but that it was the last place that I found solace. I needed a place of comfort.

  Savannah was a pretty short drive from Atlanta- at least for a woman that has driven from New Jersey to California twice. So we packed up and headed south. I had been down there for three days and my vision was not getting any clearer. Then we headed down to the beach, which once again was the highlight of my trip. It was serene and I could really focus and think.

Dj managed to have a great time and enjoyed our trip to Savannah after all as we took in all the major sights including the intrusion of jellyfish at the beach. As we embarked on our 4 hour drive back to Atlanta I received a call from my daughter.

My daughter Jenae, who I affectionately call my twin, had never seen me in such a place of frenzy, of feeling lost and not in control. She was tired of watching me being frustrated with my circumstance. She was truly concerned about her mother so she stepped up to the plate and encouraged change.

"Hi mom, she began, I booked you for a photo shoot tomorrow. You have to be ready and be on-set by 10am!" she announced.

"What are you talking about Jenae?" Now, I was irritated.

"A photo shoot for what?", "What's on-set?" I questioned.

Jenae proceeded to say "It's a stock portfolio shoot. I submitted your information to the director and they loved your look, Mom. You'll be portraying a mother in a family shoot."

"OMG, I'm coming from the beach and my hair is a mess. I can't believe you did this to me. This is so last minute." "Ugh!"

Now this idea didn't come out of left field, my daughter was a working model so she knew how to find work in the industry. Needless to say, I took her lead and went to the photo shoot. Feeling anxious and nervous as if butterflies were about to fly right out of my stomach. I was doing something I'd never done before. Even though being pushed out of my comfort zone was exhilarating I began to second guess myself as I approached the house (the set). I was having a conversation with myself while driving that went something like this;

"Will someone please tell me what I'm doing here?"

"It's not too late to turn around is it?"

"I know; I could call out sick, like I did in the corporate world". Damn, none of these ideas were working for me because I knew better. I'm a professional and there is no way that I'd back out of a commitment. The show must go on with

"ME", I was an absolute basket case, ready for action.

    I was pleasantly surprised to arrive at a mini mansion to find the big spot lights, cameras, crew, director, and photographer prepared and ready to shoot. My new family for the day was a handsome husband, rock-star son and model-type daughter. They say "fake it til' you make it" and so I did. I played it as if I'd been modeling for years. We took a variety of shots in the backyard reminiscing over iced tea, then in the front yard walking down the street, and finally preparing for a family trip; I was having a fabulous time, but then it began to rain. My hair was in a curly weave bob style and like I said I'd been at the beach so it was not in the best condition.

Photo 1 Tybee Island, Savannah, Georgia

    The stylist approached me and said, "With this rain your hair may begin to poof out, right?" "Is there any way you can pull your hair back into a ponytail?" "Sure" I said. Perturbed at first, but then I pulled the hair back into a make-shift ponytail and kept shooting. I posed like a pro. "Open the mail box and pretend you're reaching for the mail" the photographer yelled. And so I did. I was acting out the images from a created concept on paper and I pulled it off. My newly formed family and I nailed the shoot! Talk about excited, no one was more excited than when we received our checks for $150.00 for a 2-hour photo shoot. Now this was a job I could tolerate. I eventually found out that a "stock portfolio shoot" is a concept shoot, and that

those photos are entered into a database (stock) for banks, insurance, medical, health and other type of companies to search through for their commercial ads, websites, and social media. I left the location excited beyond words and very proud of my performance on "the set".

As I drove home I called my husband, "Guess what? I got paid $150 for a 2 hour shoot, what you think about that?" "I'm proud of you babe", hubby stated. Now I was eager to talk with my daughter about more prospects. I'd crossed a barrier, stepped out of my comfort zone and into an unknown arena that I enjoyed immensely. This was the beginning of my journey. I finally felt empowered!

FYI:

Stock photos (stock photography) are professional photographs of common places, landmarks, nature, events or people that are bought and sold on a royalty-free basis and can be used and reused for commercial design purposes (example: bank commercials or real estate ads); much different than a high-fashion or print model photo shoot.

Photo 2 Stock Portfolio Shoot

My Take Away from T.D. Jakes: Mind, Body and Soul:

Empowerment: Giving power to (someone); owning power; to own power; the acceptance of what you are able to control

- This is what I can control
- The one thing we can control is our mind
- Important to surround yourself with positive people and be conscious; somehow the two will ground you

Quotes to "Keep It Movin":

"The empowered woman is powerful beyond measure and beautiful beyond description."
~Dr. Steve Maraboli

"Refocusing on what you do want will take you in the direction of what you want."
~Joe Vitale

"Have the utmost respect for whatever artistic endeavors you wish to pursue and execute brilliantly. With the arts, people tend to think it's okay to skip the work."
~Beverly Bond, Founder/CEO Black Girls Rock! Inc.

CHAPTER 2

Extra-Extra: KEEP IT MOVIN'

*"**Keep it Moving**- A figure of speech for "continued forward movement"*

"Hap-py birth-day to you, Hap-py birth-day to you, Hap-py birth-day Dear Came-ron, Hap-py birth-day to you!" and everyone began to clap and cheer.

Yes, I just sang Happy Birthday to Cameron Diaz! In-credible! Not only that, my cohorts and I managed to finagle our way into being served a piece of birthday cake (the only background artists to receive any as far as I know).

I guess you're wondering how on earth I was singing the birthday song to Cameron Diaz, huh? Well, my daughter gave me all the casting agency contacts for background artist or extras (as they refer to it in Atlanta) and showed me how to submit to them and I did. Little did I know that my first submission would land me a job in the movie "What to Expect When You're Expecting" featuring Cameron Diaz, Jennifer Lopez and Elizabeth Banks. Elated and overjoyed at the opportunity I confirmed and booked my role.

I was booked as an "audience member" for 5 days and subsequently booked additional days as a "pregnant woman". As I read the confirmation email it seemed pretty basic with all the details of the call time, place, directions, parking and the "do's & don'ts" while filming. There was a lot for me to read and decipher that's for sure. I admit I was annoyed by the fact that we were not allowed cell phones, and I obliged (the first few times, (wink).

However, the one thing that stuck out most was it said to be prepared for a 12-14 hour day. What the hell! Admittedly so, I was NOT thrilled with the possibility of being onset that long for 5 straight days but the anticipation of the unknown kept me focused.

The first thing to do was to figure out my wardrobe. Casting said to wear your best choice and bring 4-5 completely different outfits including shoes to show to the costumes department. Excuse me, were they taking me on another mini vacation? Seriously, that's a lot of clothes to drag along and I was pretty sure my son wasn't booked to carry my bag.

Photo 3 DawnAngela ; Costume for "What to Expect When You're Expecting"

On top of that the instructions seemed to be in code; park at this location and then transportation will take you to "extras holding." What are extras holding and why am I being transported? I thought to myself. Nervous, anxious, and unclear of what to expect (no pun intended) upon my arrival, I followed the instructions to a "T". The directions instructed us to follow the yellow signs marked "Extras Parking" and sure enough as I approached the streets leading to the location itself, I saw all of these yellow signs showing me the way. Eventually I found myself at an old Home Depot that had been revamped into a movie set. Amazing! I was in awe as I walked through the parking lot seeing the actor's trailers and all. I entered into "extras holding" and was overwhelmed by the hundreds of people in the building. This was what was known as a "cattle call" for extras. I was just a little peon amongst hundreds of men & women for this 5 day shoot.

After checking in with casting, garment bag in tow, I shuffled around to find a seat before they were all taken.

"Is anyone sitting here?" I asked this guy at a table.

"No, go ahead and sit", he said. "Thank you" and I grabbed a seat, settled in, filled out the voucher and other miscellaneous paperwork and then went to get in line with the costumes department. Luckily for me the outfit I was wearing was approved.

I remember the wardrobe lady saying, "Your dress is perfect! You've made life a little bit easier for me today. You're set for the week."

"Wait, did she just say I was set for the week?" I thought to myself. Yes, they were shooting the same scenes for the entire week and I had to wear the same dress over and over and over again (20-Minute Woolite Dryer sheets were quickly put into action). Breakfast was waiting for us. Oatmeal, grits, cereal, bagels, bacon, fruit, juice and more. This was much more than I had expected, I grabbed a plate began to pile it on. Returning to my seat a lady asked if she could join me at the table. I welcomed the company.

"What's your name?" I managed to ask while stuffing my face. "Summer, and yours?" she said soft spoken. We quickly learned that this was both of our first day on set as "extras". OMG, we had so much in common it was ridiculous. We took our first steps as a background artist together for the next several days (and beyond). Amazed at what it takes to make movies, the crew, the cast, the chaos behind the scenes, the rules & regulations for us extras, there was so much to process but I immersed myself into it all. After a couple of hours we were finally taken to set and placed in our seats. There I met Ecckles (who today I affectionately refer to as my son from another mother), he is a young man, about my daughters' age with so much energy and joy busting out the seams; honestly who could not become his friend? He joined forces with Summer and I and together we worked through our first film, what a wonderful experience.

I could barely contain myself. I couldn't believe that I'd been placed on the front row of the scene, right in front of the actors "marks". Yes, this was going to be a great 5 days and it only got better. The gods showed no mercy, and I ended up working 14-16 hour days. Delirium began to set in by the 10th hour each day to the point where the three of us could barely contain ourselves. Our cues from the assistant director seemed to get lost in translation but somehow we made it through to the end-of the-day .

Now remember, there were nearly 200 extras cast for this movie, so imagine the lines of everyone so desperately trying to escape when it was finally time to sign out for the evening. This was going to add another hour before I could finally go home. Ugh! But still, all was good and I was happy to do it again the next day.

The making of this movie gave me the opportunity to sing Happy Birthday to Cameron Diaz, be in a scene with Elizabeth Banks, and graciously be introduced to Dwyane Wade (gulp!). I was also in the trailer for the film prior to its hitting the theatres; but the highlight for me was actually seeing myself (as a pregnant woman with fake belly) on the Big Screen! Can you imagine that? I'm sitting there watching the movie and there I am big as day, literally. (Giggling) Not bad for a girl's first experience as an "extra"!

Working as an extra not only provided income but it was also a networking opportunity. Every day on set was an adventure. I'd never know who I'd meet, cultural background, working status, etc. I learned most about the industry through word of mouth and connections via other background artist or crew. If it weren't for us "schooling" one another we'd be running around in circles. Also, friendships were made. I mean after 14-16 hour days on set you get to know each other real well, and some of those ties will be long lasting.

Photo 4 Movie Trailer for "What to Expect When You're Expecting" 2012

After talking to people onset I soon realized that my awesome first time experience was not the norm. I'm grateful I surpassed some of the negative experiences; otherwise I may not have pursued other gigs. Quickly I was also made to understand that age wasn't particularly my friend in this industry either. When I submitted for projects (Ex. seeking women ages 40-50 to be high society at a charity event) and gave my exact age I'd never get booked.

One day I asked a casting director, "Why am I not getting booked on anything that I submit to you?" He said, "Because you appear younger than what we're looking for". "That's not fair. So what am I supposed to do?" I exclaimed. "Go for younger" he replied and walked away. Then I spoke to other ladies same age and was given a tip, to begin submitting according to my "age range" which is typically 10 years back from your true age (if you can easily pass for said age). You didn't have to tell me twice, so I became 33 at 43, 34 at 44 and so on and so forth. I began to get work on a regular basis to the point that I sometimes double-booked myself which is a no-no! I actually later confirmed the age controversy with an agent who said that all actors work within an age range so I was doing the right thing.

There's much, much more to being a background artist than standing around. We bring life to the movie, TV or talk show. There's even more to being a working actor. It takes time, talent and honing your craft. Success doesn't come overnight therefore I chose to begin acting classes to test the waters. I soon found myself favored most times I was on set. I may have been booked to be mere background for the day; however, many times the director or assistant director would pull me aside and give me specific direction or place me to work directly with the actors.

By being humble and understanding my role I managed to book numerous roles, such as "Flight" with Denzel Washington who is as handsome up-close as he is on screen, also starring Don Cheadle who I had the pleasure of sitting next to in my scene for 2 days while sharing snacks with him too; "Last Vegas" starring Michael Douglas, Robert De Niro, Kevin Kline all of whom I personally met and who were very charming, and of course, Morgan Freeman who I had the pleasure of dancing with while taping a scene; also Romany Malco of "Last Vegas" was hilarious as we took pictures together and he introduced me and my girl, Kylie, to 50 Cent who made a cameo appearance in the film.

I can go on and on about the celebs I've encountered throughout the years and have good and bad stories to tell; however the point is our experiences are ours to own and that much I've truly done.

Don't get it twisted! All experiences aren't good experiences and there were some doosies! Working as an extra is just like working any other job-you're hired for a purpose and if you don't meet their criteria when you submit to the casting, well, you're simply not hired. Days and weeks could go by with no work being offered. Patience is a virtue; unfortunately my patience was wearing thin. Deciding not to sit around and twiddle my thumbs waiting for the phone to ring, I ventured into uncharted waters. How else would I determine if acting was for me without dipping into some classes?

The hard work began with on-camera audition, monologue and voice-over classes. Each class was very different and each class required my utmost attention.

Day 1 of on-camera auditions class we were quickly given "sides" which are actual scripts. In this case, we were working with current film and television scripts that would be used to have mock auditions. The purpose of the "sides" and mock auditions are to help us develop formable tools needed to be able to confidently walk into a TV or film casting like a pro. We learned how to break-down the "sides" line-by-line. Believe it or not, there is a guideline to understanding the script and your character's role in the scene. Every line on that script—from the title of the film to the episode number—has meaning. I hadn't understood the process prior to that.

Script Technique tips:

1. Why is the scene in the movie?
2. What is happening for me (my character) in the scene?
3. Personalize what is happening for me (my character) in the scene.
4. Understand your 1st moment and thought (before scene) & Understand your last moment and thought (end scene)
5. Beats and transitions (typically the script doesn't have punctuation or if so it may not be fitting so, separate lines with punctuation before trying to learn the script)

Man, this class was no joke! Embarrassed the first time I was in the audition chair, the "hot seat" if you will. I came to find that there was no progress in feeling embarrassed—I was only hurting my advancement as an actor. I soon pushed that feeling aside and learned to be in the moment of each scene and not concern myself with others that were in the room. It is imperative that if I amount to be a professional actor I should have a specific technique that I can count on for each audition. If you define yourself and develop a defined way of working, then whatever is for you will be for you. Once you've developed a solid technique that works for you than you'll be able to "hit the mark" at your auditions each and every time.

Also I was introduced to the two most used and long standing acting techniques, the Meisner technique and Method acting. One form or the other works best for actors but they are definitely different styles of technique and you cannot mix the two.

Method acting, also known as the Strasberg Method is when an actor tries to replicate the life circumstances, mannerisms and emotional feelings of the character she/he portrays, so as to give realism, legitimacy and dramatic strength to her/his performance.

Using emotional and affective memory. This is using past emotions to generate current emotions. These actors typically get so engrossed in their characters that many have been deemed "hard to work with". Robert DeNiro & Daniel Day Lewis are prime examples of a brilliant Method actor. For me, I did not connect with the Strasberg Method. This technique was definitely not for me because I have bad recall of things of the past and therefore it was a stretch for me to bring emotion from past events that may or may not have happened.

The Meisner technique on the other hand emphasizes being in the "moment". It teaches us to listen and respond truthfully to other actors in the moment. Meisner creates the ability for actors to have spontaneity, make strong choices, DO rather than pretend to do and work from our gut without dredging up personal and potentially damaging images. I loved this class! It broke me to a certain extent. Meaning, I learned a great deal about myself, that I was able to relate and be in the moment with another actor. I was pushed into a place of "truth".

Being in the moment and stating what you feel at that very minute was more appealing and genuine to me as an actor. Nobody would be confused as to my state of mind because I was telling you "like it tis'", as my father would say. I must say, I was rudely awakened when a fellow actor (during a scene and in the moment) called me out.

She said "you're fake". I said "I'm fake".

She said "I don't know you". I said, "You don't know me." (Said with an attitude)

She said "you hide behind your pretty face." I said "I hide behind my pretty face".

I said "you're weak". She said "I'm weak".

Then I said "you're a hater". She said, "I'm a hater".

And this dialogue continued until the instructor stopped us in our tracks. We were getting nowhere (in the scene) because we both shut down. I was pissed at the fact someone had called me "fake" and basically saying I was using my "pretty face" for advantage.

You get the gist of the exercise, don't you? Since I know that we were speaking "in the moment", I understand that this is how she perceived me to be. It irked me a lot but at the same time I maintained my position and/or character in that moment.

Photo 5 Movie Trailer for "Last Vegas" 2013

    A few seasoned Meisner technique actors are Sandra Bullock, Naomi Watts and James Caan. Basic instincts and reacting to the moment for me was more real than anything I'd studied prior. Sanford Meisner defined acting as "living in imaginary circumstances", and that my dear I feel I've conquered as a model & actress.

    One thing I learned is that there is no "magic formula" to acting. And there is always time for "firsts" in our lives. Don't be afraid to take the challenge, the plunge and just "go for what you know". Put your best foot forward and "DO".

FYI:

BACKGROUND ARTIST (BG) and/or Extra: Movie BGs/extras are actors hired to populate a scene and give a brief performance. By definition, extras have few (very rarely) to no spoken lines; however, the contribution they bring to the film is extremely valuable and absolutely necessary to make the story believable. It has been said that background cast members often require little or no acting experience. This however is not true. Any type of unrealistic portrayal must include some form of imagination and acting.

EXTRAS HOLDING: This is the area where production has you sign in, sign out and stay when you are not being used. You will return here to sign out and get your copy of your voucher. This is where you remain during the day, so PA's can find you when they need to place you in a scene.

ON SET: This is where the film is being recorded, and your chance to work side by side with the actors.

My Take Away from T.D. Jakes: Mind, Body and Soul:

- Socializing will give you the opportunity to network with individuals who may have a job or may not have had a job but because there's something about you that they like they'll keep you in mind.

- More times than not people hire people that they know and they can't know you if you stay frustrated and stay at home.

Quotes to "Keep it Movin":

"There's always something to suggest that you'll never be who you wanted to be. Your choice is to take it or keep on moving."
~Phylicia Rashad

"Don't dwell on what went wrong. Instead, focus on what to do next. Spend your energies on moving forward toward finding the answer."
~Denis Waitley

"Get out of your head and into your body"
~Kristen Shaw, Acting Coach

CHAPTER 3

Zumba: INSPIRED

*"**Inspire**: to make (someone) want to do something; to give (someone) an idea about what to do or create; to cause (something) to happen or be created; to cause someone to have (a feeling or emotion)"*

"I'm going to the gym!" I yelled as I was walking out the door.

I needed to get rid of this excess energy. It's been a week since I've been on set and I was getting bored again. Staying still is not my style. I pumped out 20 minutes on the treadmill and then I went on to Zumba class. I'd been doing Zumba at home via DVDs for a couple months and really loved the workout so I decided to go the classes at my local gym. In case you're unfamiliar, Zumba is a Latin-dance inspired workout that involves dance and aerobic elements. Zumba's choreography incorporates hip-hop, soca, samba, salsa, merengue, mambo and some martial arts. I'm a big fan of Latin music, always have been.

    Four routines in and I was feeling good. My mind was clear and damn, my favorite routine was about to jump off. Being that I was in my own world (inside my head), I didn't realize I kind of took over the class. The instructor just went with it.

Photo 6 Zumba Certification

"Girl, you worked us to death today! Great class" I exclaimed after. "No, you had a great class today", the instructor said jokingly. Smiling with a smirk, I took a sip of my water, said "bye" put on my sweat jacket and bounced. I'd been going to classes twice a week and doing the DVDs every day, I had become addicted to the Zumba movement. It was exhilarating. My sister-in-law was doing Zumba too. She had taken the instructor class and was on me every day to become an instructor too. What was my hesitation? My age and I was afraid, simple as that.

Who becomes a Zumba instructor at 43 years old? Well many I soon found out but at this moment age actually was a factor for me. With my personality you'd think everything came easy for me but it hasn't. Branching into new areas is not always easy for me especially when doing them alone. My husband, kids and friends were my crutch. As long as someone else was involved with me, I was set. I felt secure. Pretty strange, because most people view me as a leader, and I was a leader in many given circumstances depending on my headspace. However, still on the path of finding my niche, and, my passion; after that class that day I was inspired to take the instructor course on my own.

"Babe, Babe, Babe, where are you?" I yelled throughout the house. Still sweaty and stinky I found my hubby and son working out. "I'm going to do it, take the Zumba instructor classes."

Son laughing, "first of all you can't dance, second of all you have no rhythm". Now mind you, this kid is "team mom" most of the time, but him admitting that I had any type of skill was not going to happen. I signed up for a one-day class to take place in the next two weeks.

Have you ever been so excited that you couldn't sleep? The class couldn't come soon enough for me. It was in such a demand that all the dates were taken in Atlanta. I had to travel to

Woodstock, GA for the instruction. Didn't bother me none I was on my way to becoming an instructor. It was a 6 hour class and if you survived it, you were certified. Whew, Jose', the instructor was too cute; he came from Florida to teach the class. He didn't waste any time; we started with stretching (the Zumba way). With Zumba there's always constant movement. Everything was cool until we started doing moves I had never done before. My son was right; I had NO rhythm in that moment. By the time I turned around everyone else was facing in the other direction. Oh well, I played it off and made it through. The class was grueling yet fun at the same time. We were on our feet dancing for 5 of the 6 hours, and was exhausted. Jose', two assistants and a room full of 30 women managed to make it through 6 hours of training, ending the day with a choreographed routine that we all had to pass to be certified. "YES! My routine was salsa" that was easy for me. Needless to say I emerged a certified Zumba instructor. I had achieved my goal (minus the two nails that had fallen off both big toes)!

Now that I was an instructor the first for me to do was to post my bio on the Zumba Fitness website so establishments and/or individuals searching for instructors could make contact. Next up, I had to create my very own sequence of choreographed routines. On fire and anxious to get started my mind went into overdrive thinking of the lineup of music for my routines. I was dancing from sun up to sun down creating my own routines. Writing the moves down verse by verse; going over them over and over again was a thrill. I couldn't stop. My family was sick-n-tired of me playing Latin-music all day long. When I finally looked at myself my body, my shape was at its best. I couldn't figure out the perfect song to use to choreograph for the beginning of my routine. Of course, the first dance is always for stretching your muscles so I knew it had to be upbeat and I wanted something other than Latin-music.

Photo 7 Members of Zumba Instructors for performance at WNBA Atlanta Dream's Game

As I was driving home one day, pumping my Jill Scott CD, my favorite song came on "So In Love" by Jill Scott ft. Anthony Hamilton. This was my "happy" song. It put me in a perfect place every time I heard it. This was the song. I created the dance in my mind on the way home. Got home and perfected it. By the end of the day I was in performance mode. Every time one of my children or my hubby walked in the door, they were required to watch me perform and, I actually encouraged my hubby to perform the routine with me. Actually, I dedicated the salsa Latin-dance to him. My CD was complete, now I just needed to find a studio or gym to work within. I received several calls due to the website to teach and I taught one class alongside my girlfriend which was a fun experience.

Noticing the ladies having some trouble with the technique during my regular class at my gym, I began to assist in that area. I mean you can't really enjoy yourself if you're two steps behind and feeling less than confident. Even though some ladies may not have been on point, they were having fun because they now at least knew the steps. Weeks later I was approached by one of the ladies after class, "Thanks Dawn, she began I've been watching you since you joined our class and

I'm so excited that you became an instructor to the point that you've inspired me to do the same". "What? I had no idea, Thank You" as I gave her a big hug. She laughed and said "now see if you can teach here, you're so good." I realized in that moment that you never know who's watching and who you may affect by just being yourself. BTW, she was 52 years old. My sister-in-law and I were contemplating opening our own studio. I have a cousin who is a Zumba instructor in California; not only was she an instructor but she was in the process of establishing her own studio. We decided to give her a call. We set up a conference call and were inspired even more to pursue the dream.

Wait, but was this my dream? Nope, it wasn't my dream; it was my hobby, my exercise, my outlet, my place of calm. And I was okay with that. So okay that I joined with a group of female Zumba instructors and performed Zumba's "Caipirinha" during half-time at one of the WNBA Atlanta Dreams basketball games. This was the conclusion of me pursuing Zumba as a business. I had been inspired, my fears were conquered and I took the steps needed to move forward and toward a place of self-confidence. In taking those steps I was also unknowingly an inspiration to someone else. Breathtaking!

My Take Away from T.D. Jakes: Mind, Body and Soul:

- Keep a positive perspective.

- Don't allow circumstances to overtake you otherwise they will.

Quotes to Keep it Movin':

"Let your dreams be bigger than your fears & your actions louder than your words."
~Unknown

"What God intended for you goes far beyond anything you can imagine."
~Oprah Winfrey

"To be inspired is great; to inspire is incredible."
~Unknown

CHAPTER 4

A Thin Line: BALANCE

*"**Balancing Act:** an attempt to cope with several often conflicting factors or situations at the same time"*

Grueling long hours working on set as a background artist, along with two classes per week, one during the day (acting), and the other at night (voice-over), both 3 hours each, was a juggling act. Incorporating that along with trying to manage family, exercise and taking care of myself in the process was not going very smoothly.

I pride myself with being a very organized and together woman. Anyone would tell you that I'm a stickler for details. For some reason my skill for prioritizing had fallen out the window. Yes, I got it twisted! Somehow I got caught up in the hype of the industry life. Seeking gigs, networking, and working consumed every area of my life. Let me explain.

We all know that Facebook is an online social networking service; however, the use of it can be destructive to a relationship. For instance, I have two Facebook accounts, one for family and the other for business. The business account was created to keep my personal and business separate as well as a means for me to connect with the casting agencies for jobs. Believe it or not, in Georgia, Facebook "FB" is where most if not all the casting agencies post jobs for extras. Not only that, there are extra casting "groups" on Facebook that I joined as well. With Facebook comes "FB friends". Yes, in order to network you have to become connected with others in the same community as your business.

Photo 8 Punta Cana Photo Shoot

The entertainment arena is not gender specific and therefore my FB friends were both male and female. At the start, my FB friends were those I met onset and at different networking events, then I began to receive FB "requests" from the unknown. You never know the intentions behind a "FB request" but it didn't matter to me as I was building my network. On occasion, I'd get "inbox" messages from guys asking for my number or inquiry as to my marital status, those were ignored or I graciously stated, "my husband would not appreciate" and left it at that. The more I established myself and became connected the more communications were had on Facebook. Although my intentions were business and/or just chatting with fellow actors; my hubby did not appreciate the conversations at all. Stubborn me, instead of understanding his point of view as a husband I was angered because I saw no harm. In my eyes, am I only supposed to communicate or work with female agents, actors, photographers, producers, etc.? That is unrealistic in my world. The overall picture for me was that he was stifling my walk, my growth and any potential lead to a better opportunity. Of course, I was incorrect in my assessment because my hubby is my greatest supporter but at the same time it has been difficult for him to grasp the world I've now entered. As he tends to say, "Dawn, not everyone has your best interest at heart" or "everything that glitters ain't gold". Many arguments and conversations later, we've come to an understanding and, I too, had a statement "all connections ain't good connections".

Admittedly, I'd be up to the wee hours of the morning submitting myself for jobs. There were days when I would be on Facebook all damn day.

"Hey babe how was work?" I asked as my hubby walked in the house. "Okay", as he delicately kissed my lips. "You have until 8pm to be on that computer then come watch TV with me" he proclaimed. "No problem!" I said. Time marched on. "Babe, are you joining me, the show is about to start"? "Yes, give me 5 minutes." 5, 10, 15, 30 minutes went by and I'd forgotten my commitment to simply watch TV with my hubby. Little commitments broken are BIG commitments to the person on the receiving end. This wasn't the first time.

"I can't, I don't have time, wait, maybe tomorrow", "in a minute". Time and time again I would utter these words, unknowingly in my family's eyes blowing them off while in pursuit of my dreams.

Maybe you've been there, feeling like you've given so much of yourself to the family, with no accomplishments to call your own. So when the opportunity shows itself and it's your chance to shine, well, you do everything you can do to make it happen. That's a place I know all too well. Of course, I'd give my life for my family; however, for me, the emotion of self-sacrifice was real.

There'd been a shift in priorities. A Flip-Flop! Hubby had "signed on" agreeing to me not going back to the 9-5 and this was MY TIME, a new chapter in our lives. You might say I was on the receiving end of his self-sacrifice and for a moment I felt like Cinderella.

Back on the block, working consistently in an industry that I'm very passionate about, getting paid, working my charm, my skills, and on my own schedule was a thrill. Stadium long days, caregiver nights, not enough sleep, and don't forget the hubby! He was my #1 supporter and understood there'd be a little craziness; however, he didn't know how much.

Photo 9 Punta Cana Photo Shoot with Hubby

I thrive to be fully present in every moment- to be really connected to whatever I'm doing, even if it's just popcorn and a movie with the family.

Every day is a juggling act and although not perfectly, over time I've learned to put things in writing and on a calendar for "all" to view. I thought "date night" was a misnomer but I found that in order for a relationship to sustain, especially in the industry I was in pursuit of, you've got to pencil it in, and truly make that time for the people who are dear to your heart. Without faith I'd be lost; luckily faith found me and I'm good. My quest for independence, my vigor to achieve my goals, and my drive to live an awesome life forced me to a place of balance.

Take Away from T.D. Jakes: Mind, Body and Soul:

- Keep a positive perspective
- Faith is a critical component in the process; it stimulates your inner heart

Quotes to Keep it Movin':

"Mistakes are a fact of life. It is the response to the error that counts."
~Nikki Giovanni

"Women need real moments of solitude and self-reflection to balance out how much of ourselves we give away."
~Barbara de Angelis

"My point is life is about balance. The good and the bad. The highs and the lows. The Pina and Colada."
~Ellen Degeneres

CHAPTER 5

Road Map: DEVELOPMENT

*"**Development:** the act or process of growing or causing something to grow or become larger or more advanced"*

Privileged to have traveled throughout the states and abroad in my early years and beyond; has afforded me life lessons that I may not otherwise have known.

Having been an Air Force brat growing up we moved here and there, but for the most part I was raised in two places/two phases. The breakdown: Elementary & Middle schools-San Jose, CA; High School & college- Sacramento, CA. The significance of the phases are important to understand.

Phase one, elementary school. Well, for the most part I was either the sole or one of two African-American kids in the classroom. That alone really did not bother me—not that I recall—and I really never thought about it until I found old school pictures. I was shy during my early years, and didn't really understand the racial tension during the 70s because I'd lived abroad in Panama prior to California. I do recall, one favorite female teacher, whose name escapes me but she really looked out for me and made me comfortable in my new surroundings by including me in swim parties, escorting me out of the classroom at the end of day to see that I was safe.

    As a young tot, I thought everyone was supposed to be my friend. I didn't understand why it was such a big deal to others that my neighborhood best friend Becky was white (Caucasian). I was taught to treat everyone with respect, treat them as you would want them to treat you. None of this seemed to bother me as my parents saw to it that I was involved in every extracurricular activity that I showed interest. My weekends were consumed with ballet, jazz and tap dancing lessons.

    Tap was my favorite of them all. You should've seen me this one Saturday recital. All dolled up with a little make-up, lip gloss and some very rosy cheeks. My costume was red and yellow that of a "chickadee". I'll never forget it. I thought I was the cutest thing walking that day other than my cousin who I believe was a "sheep". Who knows what the performance was about -all I know is I tapped my behind off. I felt like I was the center of attention. Of course that wasn't the case but you know little girls when we're dressed up all focus should be on us. On top of that I was in a local baton twirling troop that performed in parades and won several performance medals. The elementary era was a good one I must say.

      Middle school was a time of growth, social clubs, "clicks", trying to fit in, being obnoxious & hard-headed, and first love. Keeping up with the marching band I became a "flag girl" and traveled both northern and southern California. Our band was one of the best and we won numerous trophies over the years. Going from elementary to middle school is no easy fete. New school, new friends and some old ones, new teachers, and a new type of schedule were intimidating. No longer the big 5th grader, now its back on the lowest totem pole you could find, 6th grade. We looked like peons compared to the other kids. I soon found my "crew" that stuck together through 8th grade. First school dance, first kiss, first crush, and just a slew of emotions throughout these years. These were fun times.

      There was a point of identity crisis; well, I wouldn't go that far. The community in which we lived I would say was pretty diverse therefore the school consisted of Mexican, African-American, Filipino, and Caucasians. Even though, clearly we sectioned ourselves into groups we also wanted to gel with each other. There were days when I'd dress like a Cholas in my Dixie's, or baggy jeans, tank-tops (aka the wife beater) and thought I was Mexican. I believe my nickname was "La Angel". Back then everyone was "La" something or other. Then there were days when I hung with my Filipino friends and conformed just the same. Always maintaining who I am, it was the dress and style that drew me to change NOT wanting to be someone other than African-American DawnAngela. Looking back its funny to me and I wish I had the pictures to show.

     My parents were pretty strict. "Do you have your permission slip?" a friend made fun as we jumped on the bus to go to the mall. "Real funny", I laughed. At 13 we were catching buses to the mall and the movies almost every Saturday and definitely during the summertime. I remember the bus fare being $.25 cents and was highly upset when it went up to $.50. I had some nerve being upset, right? I believe a one-way fare now is $2. Any who, there was nothing like riding the bus with your friends, of course with the plan of meeting your "boo" at the other end of the route. I'm not the only one out there whose meeting place was the mall. And don't forget the roller skating rink, don't get me started on that because I can tell you some great stories but I won't. ☺ Although my parents were strict to a certain extent they allowed me to learn by trial and error.

Somewhere in between, my military-socialite dad began college at 40 years old and graduated at the top of his class, then was called into the ministry. Sure enough, he was ordained a minister of which I was very proud. Definitely a daddy's girl, I knew whatever he sought for us to do as a family would be for the better. We were off to a new city where my dad would become the Pastor of his own church. I was now a "Preachers Kid (P.K.)"!

A young, tall, skinny little eighth-grader leaves her friends she'd known since grammar school, her bestie (cousin) and her boyfriend. To me the world was coming to an end. We were set to move over the summer so I could begin H.S. in the fall in Sacramento. Promises were made with the girls, "friends for life"! Tears were shed, "I'll love you forever", he said. I know, dramatic but real. Leaving San Jose behind to embark on a new life and new friends was terrifying, especially entering 9th grade where kids already have established friendships.

Phase two, high-school. Circa 1980, Two-story home, a newly developed subdivision and the H.S. was in walking distance from the house. Nervous was not the word but I trotted the fertile ground every day to JFK. The first couple of weeks were okay. I made friends slowly. Being the "new girl on the block" there was "hater-ation" from the girls and "necks breakin'" from the guys. Once again I was being labeled, this time; it was "stuck-up and conceited". Yes, I was the girl who thought she was too cute and better than everyone else because of the brand name clothes, the car dad drove (a Bonneville but everyone mistook it for a Cadillac) and the house we lived in.

My mother taught me to carry myself with grace, be poised, speak when spoken to, and know who you are and where you came from. I was no better than anyone else, unfortunately for me, nobody cared. These girls were ruthless! I was bullied and threatened for the first part of the year. Quickly, I smartened up and began to make friends; however, those friends were mostly guys because the girls from the jump didn't like me. Of course being friends with the basketball team only enhanced the drama. The girls were jealous. Mind you I was still holding on to my boyfriend back in San Jose and not really giving anyone else the time of day. I was in a no win situation. I became friends with a couple of the toughest girls in school (really it was their persona). I knew I'd be safe when they were around but when they weren't that's when trouble began. Skipping class was a norm just to avoid being cornered in the hallway.

My recluse was the girl's restroom. One day I walked into the smoky, grungy restroom, went into the stall to pass time waiting for the bell to ring and much to my surprise, there was "hate mail" written all over the stall (not one stall but all four). "I'm gonna get you bitch", "You're dead", "I'm going kick your ass" and one had an entire paragraph about how I stole her man that I didn't even know. Running with the wrong crowd, smoking-who could concentrate on school work? I managed to weather the storm but 9th grade academically was a total nightmare.

You may wonder where my parents were in all of this, well, they had no idea the turmoil I'd been going through. I chose not to share it but instead endure and manage on my own. Needless to say, the following year my dad put me in an all-girls Catholic school.

Yes, I said all-girls Catholic School. I was excited actually because 1) I could get academically back on track, 2) I was going to wear a uniform and did not have to worry about wardrobe any longer, and 3) I did not have to worry about the fellas trying to "holla" all day. That would wait until after school. The boys' school was a couple blocks or so down the road {giggle}. The school was Downtown Sacramento and therefore I had to be driven to school every day. Dropped off and picked up by my father, that is until I was able to drive myself. I didn't mind. Since my dad was a preacher he'd often go to the school to speak, give a prayer at dinners and also counsel.

My dad was well liked amongst my friends, both girls & guys, pretty much a father figure. He was a pretty cool dude, God rest his soul. Dad would be our chauffeur and take me and my friends to the skating rinks, house parties, and "clubs" which were really like community center dances. He'd have the window down, sit low, lean his left arm on the window seal, steering with the other hand, music blasting and pull right in front of the building. He enjoyed trying to embarrass us.

Thought it was real funny. We'd have him pick us up around the corner from the venue at times but again he tried to be funny by pulling off as we tried to get into the car or making us chase the car to get in. Being that he was so cool often got us (him and I) into trouble with mom. I'm sure I picked up my mischievous behavior from my dad.

We'd often sneak after school to McDonald's or Taco Bell before we went home knowing that mom would have cooked dinner and we'd have to eat a little of that too. Or he'd allow me to drive a little here and there before I had my permit. Or we'd just jump in the car and drive for no other purpose than to spend father/daughter time. At the time, I didn't get the purpose, I enjoyed it but as I grew older I understood that this was his way of getting to know his daughter and sowing seeds into my life. He was my best friend. My subsequent years of H.S. were great-I met my life-long best friend of whom we'll go down as being the life of the parties. Seriously, my three years in Catholic school I can't complain, graduating in 1985.

The college years, at least the beginning was met with some uncertainty. I didn't see college as being a part of my program. Unsure of what I wanted to do I went ahead and applied to several local colleges and was pleasantly accepted to a few. I chose to go to UC Davis, Davis, CA which was just a 20-30 minute drive away. I moved into the dorms and there made friendships that have carried over until this day. Year one, hell-on-wheels! I must say that there was more party than pen to the pad. As a matter of fact, let's just chock this up to mistakes made and lessons learned.

Next up, 1986 marrying a sailor (my father officiated), a Navy man at the ripe old age of 19 and then moving to San Diego, CA where he was stationed. Yep, from daddy's house to hubby's house. Darryl, affectionately called "hubby" was a tech on a destroyer and therefore I didn't travel; he would go on tours for months at a time which was difficult to say the least. While hubby was in the Navy I was in college, worked as a PBX operator at a major department store and then transitioned to an IT corporation thus the beginning of my 20 year career in mortgage servicing.

Life for us was exciting I thought; my husband would always strive to make life better and/or easier for us as a family. What we had in common was our Christian values, music, movies, and a good party or concert. Outside of work I began to model doing odd print job and catalog work around the city but that quickly ended as life took me in another direction-I was going to have a baby! Baby one Jaeda Lee, born 1989 and soon after baby two, Jenae Ann born 1990. I was a busy little Navy wife-mama, one on the hip and the other hanging on the leg. I wouldn't trade a moment of time spent grooming, teaching and sharing with these girls and to now see them grow into beautiful well-rounded women, is a blessing. 9 years of service and 6 years in San Diego, hubby was offered a position outside the military. Me, securing a position as a foreclosure analyst at a law firm I was also prepared for the move, soon we were off to Virginia Beach, VA with two little girls in tow. Much to my surprise, the beach was not the same as in Cali. I was bamboozled! LOL Virginia Beach wasn't our final stop; just the beginning.

While in Virginia Beach, 1992, I tried to keep myself abreast of the latest fashions via JET and Ebony magazines. Actually I've had a subscription to them both for years another something that I picked up from my mother. That was her way of keeping in tune with our culture. I heard that the Ebony Fashion Fair Tour was going to be coming to our city and I really, really wanted to go. Although my mother had taken me when I was younger I truly couldn't remember the experience. So I put on my little black dress, hubby and I were off to the show. I was simply amazed, mesmerized, blown-away, because this was not your normal every day fashion show. The catwalk had never looked so colorful with so many variations of African-American shades of beauty. These models, women (and men) had some pizazz that I had not seen before. I was in awe from the moment the commentator stepped onto the stage. Ebony Fashion Fair was more than a fashion show it was a production that laid the ground work for women of color and most particularly for me on that day that I still had a passion for fashion, for modeling and one day I'll get there.

1994, two years later another promotion and move to Charlotte, NC (while I transferred). During the transition in between those two cities we shacked up with my in-laws for a period of time in Paterson, NJ.

Photo 10 Family Portrait 2011

    After five years in Charlotte, NC, now 1999, hubby decided it best to take a freelance job in Frankfurt, Germany. Mind you this was a great opportunity for his career path but he'd be taken abroad again, for a year. I chose to what I called "retire"! Dj was in pre-school part-time, and I home-schooled Jenae while Jaeda was in middle school. Summer break finally arrived; the kids and I were off to Germany! Talk about a whirlwind, educating experience for the girls. We must've watched the Sound of Music and Passport to Paris (Mary-Kate & Ashley Olsen) 100 times. Everywhere that the Olsen twins went in the movie, we tried to mimic and then some. The kids loved going to Euro Disney Resort. It reminded them of stateside Disney World. We played in the green at Luxembourg Gardens, the second largest public park in Paris. The Eiffel Tower, 984 feet tall was oh so breathtaking. Our past time in the states is going to the movies. At this point we were all very anxious to see a movie. While on Champs-Elysees we noticed the Cinema and were very pleased to watch "Gladiators" for the first time even in subtitles.

The highlights for me surrounded beauty and glamour. The smells from the bakery were impressive, perhaps it was "Petits fours" and "pain et confiture" that filled the air. As we walked along The Avenue des Champs-Elysées, the most famous avenue in the world I felt at home with the cinemas, theaters, cafés and luxury shops. I was drawn towards this huge, gorgeous, store that was lit up like a Christmas tree. It was Sephora, yes the French brand and cosmetic store that we all know and love in the states today but at that time it was a new vision to my eyes. We spent perhaps 2-3 hours in the joint smelling every perfume, and every cologne in the store. The kids were just as enamored as we were. I then looked in each luxury shop with big puppy dog eyes. The level of glamour was fantastic. My shopping purchases of the day were perfumes and pointy toed shoes. My first pairs of shoes from Paris, Ouais!

Then three years yet another move to Atlanta, GA in 2004 (again I transferred) and here I remain; of course, until the "next" move. Whew! I know let me allow you to catch your breath.

So what's the purpose of this long drawn out road map?

It's a recall that offers you a glimpse of my past and self-development along the way. Even though these were little stepping stones for the betterment of our lives and the experiences some good and some not so much; there were points along the way where I lost sight of myself. For me, a major part of my life was spent watching others nurture and achieve their own personal goals while I was on the sideline getting a burst of inspiration and collecting nuggets along the way. Today, I am sowing seeds into my own life, walking in faith, and taking on challenges that I may not have had in the past. I am balancing "home" while embracing the transformations that are taking place within.

My Take Away from T.D. Jakes: Mind, Body and Soul:

- Know that there is a God, something that's above you and beyond you that's able to lift you up.

Quotes to Keep it Movin':

"Today, many will break through the barriers of the past by looking at the blessings of the present. Why not you?"
~ Steve Maraboli

"Challenges are what make life interesting; overcoming them is what makes life meaningful".
~William Bennett

"Greatness is not measured by what a man or woman accomplishes, but by the opposition he or she has overcome to reach his goals."
~Dorothy Height

CHAPTER 6

The Make-Over: TRANSFORMATION

*"**Transformation:** a complete or major change in someone's or something's appearance, form, etc."*

One day in 1984, I found myself in my parent's dining room, gazing at a wall with two picture frames filled with real acrylic butterflies that were so elegantly placed onto display. This for me, was another moment for a time of reflection. These colorful butterflies have followed me from a toddler in Panama City, Panama to a teenager in California. Ever since I could remember these butterflies were a part of my life. I was enamored by them. I found solace and comfort with the butterflies.

A butterfly typically has slender thin body, long antennae with ball-like appendages on the ends. She is exquisitely beautiful in color and embellishes grace. Besides her beauty she symbolizes rebirth, change, transformation and the arrival of new life.

Imagine the butterfly, a symbol of transformation because of its impressive process of metamorphosis and emergence into her unfurling glory. Imagine your entire life changing to such an extreme you are unrecognizable at the end of the transformation. The butterfly asks us to accept the changes in our lives as casually as she does hers. The butterfly unquestionably embraces the changes of her environment and her body.

Why the fascination with butterflies? I was the "baby" of the family, so to speak, and my father always instilled in me that I was beautiful no matter what anyone else had to say. He allowed me to experience life and therefore that meant learning from both my triumphs and failures.

As women, to an extent we all feel at some point in our lives that we are "it", the "bomb" or "fine as hell" but that wasn't always the case for me. During the awkward years of puberty, I was often teased and called Olive Oil, Pippy Long Stocking, and Stick. These were not praises by any means, these were names used to reflect the thinness of my body frame. Basically, I was being chastised for my being so skinny. I laugh now and understand that there was some jealousy coming from within my camp but at the time it did hurt my feelings and made me somewhat self-conscious of my body. As I matured I grew out of that phase and began to embrace my individuality from within. Oh yes, in my mind I was the "HOTNESS!" No longer was I going to succumb to the negativity that came from others-I was going to embrace everything that was Dawn Angela.

Fast forward to the year 2011... Many of the roles I played in film were those that incorporated fashion mostly modelesque, classy and high-society types. The pattern was apparent; I was being booked not only for my talent but for my youthful appearance and beauty. I'd been so busy with acting that I'd forgotten my passion for modeling. Hmm, the combination of acting and modeling was intriguing to me.

My daughter was at the computer, "Mom, why are you standing behind me?" "Jenae, what type of website is that?" She emitted a deep sigh, "really Mom, it's Model Mayhem a place where I network with photographers and find modeling jobs". "What? Boy, times have changed since the 90's; this social media is no joke". I was ready to take the leap and reignite my passion for modeling. Taking the lead from my seed, I researched Model Mayhem, the #1 portfolio website for professional models and photographers and quickly created a profile. I began to receive messages from photographers for "Time for Print", better known as "TFP". This is where the photographer and model trade services. The photographer agrees to shoot the model at no charge, and then give her the prints for her portfolio or for her to market commercially. The model then receives the prints at no cost, in lieu of a modeling fee. That for me seemed to be a cool avenue to practice the art of modeling and build my portfolio at the same time.

Photo 11 Professional Photo Shoot Image

    One day I received an invite to a "model call" for a new liquor company looking for promotional models as well as models for several fashion magazines. The day arrived and my husband drove me to the venue. I was nervous for a couple of reasons; 1) I didn't know what to expect, I'd never gone to such a model call before, and 2) we were expected to wear a swimsuit and be photographed (shh!, I hadn't told my hubby that part). It was clear to me that I was perhaps the oldest model in the room; however what they don't know would not hurt them. There were about 30 guys and gals who auditioned wearing skinny jeans & white t-shirts. Eliminations were made after our first walk, those that remained changed into their swimsuits.

A little older, a little wiser, and perhaps a few pounds heavier (yet still skinny mini), all of my recall of the catwalk came rushing back. Walking out of the changing room in my robe I felt confident and when they called my name, I dropped the robe and stepped. All anxiety vanished and I nailed it! I was chosen to be a part of the promotional team and with that came a personal photo shoot. The top models from the shoot would be featured in the next issue of the sponsoring fashion magazine.

For an entire month before the photo shoot I shopped for the best outfits, watched YouTube videos of different shoots and simply prepared myself to the fullest. It helped that the TV series,

American's Next Top Model was on the air. Making reference to the show and the pointers given from Tyra Banks was enormously helpful. My "model bag" (everything a model needs from body foundations, make-up, undergarments to several pairs of shoes) was filled to the rim. In the days leading up to the photo shoot I became a little nervous, but I knew I was ready. Feeling extremely comfortable with my wardrobe I felt I could pull this off. When I tell you that this was the best first photo shoot experience ever, I mean it was the best first photo shoot! Baby, I was on fire! The atmosphere was jammin' as my hubby was the "DJ" for the afternoon. Three different outfits, all very different but the one that stopped everyone in their tracks was my version of Diana Ross in a fitted off the shoulder gown. Damn, I felt so sexy and in my element. Gazing at the lens, I became one with the camera as Jay-Z's and Kanye West' song, "No Church in the Wild" played in the background. Needless to say and very proud, I might add, I was in the next issue of the magazine. Rediscovery of a lost passion and having the ability to successfully transform into it was a joyous experience for me.

    Much like the butterfly, her unwavering acceptance of her metamorphosis is also a symbol of faith. The butterfly beckons us to keep the faith as we go under transitions in our lives. I've gone through several transitions in my life and in this moment I'm ready to embrace any and all transformations that may come.

Photo 12 Photo Shoot Image 2011

My Take Away from T.D. Jakes: Mind, Body and Soul:

- Faith is a critical component in the process. It really does stimulate your inner heart and to know, that there is a God, something that's above you and beyond you that's able to lift you up; sometimes when you can't lift yourself up. Many people will tell you that it was not will power but Gods power that brought them through the storm

Quotes to Keep it Movin':

"We delight in the beauty of the butterfly, but rarely admit the changes it has gone through to achieve that beauty."
~ Maya Angelou

"Your life does not get better by chance. It gets better by change."
~Jim Rohn

"Change is never easy. You fight to hold on and, you fight to let go."
~Unknown

"The word of God is transforming. It transforms the heart of the individual to make

them care more. Through the word of God people can be transformed. It's the kind of transforming love that the late Dr. Martin Luther King, Jr. preached."
~My dad, my pastor, Rev. Robert Lee Richardson

MODEL BAG:

Hair & Make-up
Face clean and free from oils
Eyelashes
Foundation
Hair washed and pre-washed

Body
Deodorant (clear)
Lotion (non-scented)
No oils/perfumes
Wash clothes, hand sanitizer
Shower gel
Mini pads

Clothing/Undergarments
Body Foundation (spanx, body shaper)
Robe
Stockings (nude & black)
Black tights
Leggings (variety of colors & lengths)
Socks (variety)
Boy Short (black)
Thongs & panties (nude, white & black, no panty lines please)
Bras (nude, white, black)

Skinny Jeans (dark blue, black, white and any other colors)
Cute all black outfit (just in case)
Heels 4 in. or higher (black, nude, silver, white, gold, pop color)
Sandals

<u>Accessories</u>
Belts
Jewelry (studs, necklaces, earrings)

<u>Miscellaneous</u>
Nail polish (nude, clear nail polish)
Tic Tacs (no gum)
Water Bottle or Gatorade & small snacks

CHAPTER 7

The Catwalk: PURPOSE

*"**Purpose:** the feeling of being determined to do or achieve something; the aim or goal of a person; what a person is trying to do, become, etc."*

My mother would often say to me, "Dawn Angela, stand up straight, pick your head up, shoulders back and walk like you have purpose." If you've ever seen someone who is a slouch they appear to lack confidence. As a model we are taught to be poised, graceful, and to walk with conviction. In order to have such you must first know who you are as a person and then exude confidence. Realizing, knowing and owning who I am as a person; a woman of intelligence, integrity, faith, and beauty is the best gift I could give myself. Another gift was learning from the best, my Mother.

I attribute my love of fashion, especially shoes to my Mom and I believe I've taken over where she's left off. As a little girl I would often play dress-up in my mother's closets, yes, that is plural she had three. Any style of dress, vintage or otherwise could be found in my mother's closet. Each dress suit had a matching pair of heels. Each outfit would have coordinating jewelry. Racks upon racks of clothes dating back to the 60's, I was in awe. I spent hours at a time trying to perfect my mother's style, her walk, her stance; she is a beautifully spirited woman who embodies grace. As Mom would say, "The steps of a good man are ordered by the LORD: and he delighteth in his way."(Psalm 37:23)

    The saying "like mother; like daughter" really doesn't fall far from the tree. Similar to my mother and I, love of fashion & shoes; my own daughters both took a liking to fashion as well. As they grew into their own personal way of style I managed to nurture them and enroll them in modeling classes.

    Finding your purpose isn't easy but when you do you must nurture it. Have you ever heard of a vision board? If you haven't you are missing out. A vision board is a collage of images, pictures and affirmations of your dreams and all of the things that make you happy. It's a great way to keep you focused and in tune with whatever gives you purpose and meaning. For me, that meant plenty of pictures of models in order to get an idea of different poses, and keeping up on current fashions. My vision board also consisted of favorite quotes to keep me motivated, pictures of family and silly sticky notes. Most importantly were my positive affirmations. I needed to project positive thoughts into my mind on a daily basis. Positive thoughts shall bring positive jobs to life.

I knew one day the acting and the modeling would merge and it did. One day as I was reading an email from my girlfriend, It stated that, "The Vampire Diaries" are looking for a model between the ages of 20-30 years. You should go for it!," she added. I know, I know, I was much older than the call had asked for, but then again nobody in the industry really knew my true age, so I submitted my photo to the casting agent and the next thing I knew I was set to meet with the director who would make the final model selection.

I was amongst 30 other models and he finally chose me. Now, I'd worked on the set of Vampire Diaries several times before as an "extra" but this time I was a "featured extra" which means I would be a part of the scene, in focus, I would be seen clearly but not have lines.

Photo 13 Vampire Diaries S/4/Ep4 "The Five"

Arriving at my call time I was pleasantly surprised because today I was actually spending the day directly with the cast. My role was to play a 100 year old witch who never aged and was a previous love interest to one of the characters. Basically it was a photo shoot of our two characters, and my character aired in Season 4/Episode 4, "The Five". This was my job for the day, who could ask for anything better.

My first fashion show in Atlanta was "F.A.B. Event (Fashion Against Bullying). Ecckles, my son from another mother (as mentioned in Ch. 2) collaborated with a team of designers, stylist, hair & make-up artist, singers and musicians, to benefit anti-bullying education & organizations.

Photo 14 First Runway Show 2011, F.A.B.

This event was my introduction to the early call times for models before a show. Always the "hurry up and wait" game. I will never understand the purpose of being at the venue 6-8 hours prior to the start of the show. Just the nature of the business I guess. I was excited as my family began to arrive in support of my big day. Being a bit nervous, I had a cocktail or two beforehand which seemed to bring calm. Everything fell into place; I dressed backstage, in the hallway actually with all the other models not really concerned with the fact that everyone's "assets" were exposed. When making these quick changes from one design to the next there's no time to sweat the small stuff. If it's an issue, my suggestion is to, put your robe in your model bag and keep it movin'.

My first appearance on the runway that night was in red and the second, purple of which I "killed it". I hit the runway with purpose and there created what would today be known as my "signature pose". It's not my best pose but was my first pose and thus has stuck with me ever since. That night, reality TV mogul, Dwight Eubanks, from the "Real Housewives of Atlanta" and who also produces fashion shows was in the audience, he approached me and my daughters to be in his next show, ergo my second fashion show, Women of

Wealth Empowerment Summit 2012. It was an honor that someone from within the modeling industry was interested in me, DawnAngela.

Photo 15 First Runway Show 2011, F.A.B.

Sometime later as I walked to the mailbox outside my home, a refreshing smell of clean was in the air after a brief down pouring of rain. Looking to the sky I saw the beautiful colors of a newly formed rainbow and at that moment I knew I was walking in my purpose and that the best of my journey was yet to come.

My Take Away from T.D. Jakes: Mind, Body and Soul:

- Keep a positive perspective

- There is a God who is there to lift you up when you can't lift yourself

Quotes to Keepin' it Movin':

> "A Woman who walks in PURPOSE doesn't have to chase PEOPLE or OPPORTUNITIES. Her LIGHT causes PEOPLE and OPPORTUNITIES to PURSUE her."
> ~Unknown

> "Where you are is a great place to be. Because from where you are, you can go anywhere you decide to go."
> ~Ralph Marston

> "A successful woman is one who can build a firm foundation with the bricks others have thrown at her."
> ~Unknown

CHAPTER 8

Model Life: ENCOURAGEMENT

*"**Encouragement:** the act of making something more appealing or more likely to happen"*

In my opinion the key to success is to be coachable. As an aspiring model one must watch, learn and listen with an open mind. If you don't think modeling is work, you are sadly mistaken! Modeling is a full time job in which you must show & prove before you can actually claim, "I am a Model". Desire and a drive to hone my craft, I sought out a runway coach. I needed a coach to reinforce what I already knew and update me to the new techniques of the day, ergo Ms. Nickee Mack of Diva Day International, Inc.

It escapes me as to just how we met, but believe me when we did meet she displayed this confidence that was simply gravitational. Her bold attitude, fierce walk, and ball of fire levels of energy were contagious. Damn, If only I had a little bit of that oomph! She's been my coach, agent, and friend for the past 2 years now. And, without those runway videos and classes, her guidance, insight, tell-tell about the "modeling game" in

Atlanta I may have given up. Her persistence and push for me to continue despite my occasional hesitation was encouraging.

In the words of Super Model, Cindy Crawford, when asked "how to get started in the modeling industry":

"If you are interested in modeling, take time to research a few agencies in the largest cities near you. Most modeling agencies have one day a week or month where they have an open call. Call the agencies and schedule an appointment. If the first agency tells you "no", keep trying! The first agency I went to wasn't sure about me and they especially wasn't sure about my mole! The agencies will give you the straight talk and let you know the best photographer for a test shoot. I'm not a big advocate of modeling schools. They will always take your money, even if they don't see any real potential.

Good luck, but also remember that there are a lot of other fulfilling jobs out there and only a tiny percentage of the people that try out for modeling are actually able to earn a living in the business."

Most models have the same sentiment with regard to modeling schools and after my own experiences with my girls, I adamantly say, "No" to anyone who may ask me.

Putting myself aside, I began to live my dreams of modeling vicariously through my daughters. My eldest, Jaeda Lee was the first to get the bug for modeling at the age of 13. Of course as a parent you want to support the desires of your kids. Countless time and dollars were spent on modeling schools that are still around today. Yes, the instructors taught etiquette, industry standards and basic walk for pageantry, but nothing that would propel her to the door of a reputable agency. She loved it and it gave her a sense of confidence.

Photo 16 Ms. Jaeda Lee on the runway

My daughter strives to be the best and practiced, practiced, practiced to the point she created her own signature walk. It wasn't until a local agency, sought interest in her and immediately signed her on as their first teen model. Honestly, Jaeda set the bar for the agency; she would out walk the adult models with perfection. She went on to join the modeling troop at Georgia State University but has thus hung up her high-heels for a marketing career. If asked to be in a show or coach runway she will most definitely come out of retirement. Ha-ha!

***

Atlanta's a little different when it comes to the fashion world, it's not the high-fashion couture of New York or swimsuit capital like Miami, but it does have its own niche which result in many-many fashion shows throughout the year. Everyone wants to be in one show or the other based upon their knowledge of the designers or the producers of the show. Also, Atlanta is also a music town, known for its Hip-Hop, and the home of several mainstream Award Shows as well as one of the top places for major movies to be filmed. There is definitely a place, and need for various types of models for promotional, runway, video, film, TV, red-carpet, and seat-filler works to name a few.

There are plenty of jobs but unfortunately, not all are paying jobs.

When you're learning the "game" it's cool to take on shows without pay because it's how you perfect your "walk"; however, as you grow into an established model or become a "signature model" for a designer your goal is to always collect that pay check. I mean, it is your "job", right? Don't settle for anything less than what you feel you're worth. Realize your worth! That reminds me, remember those funny sticky notes I would post around the house, well this sticky note, "silly rabbit tricks are for kids" was a reminder for me to keep my eyes open to the fraudulent side of the business. The ones who seem to have all the answers are the one who knows nothing at all. There are sharks in sheep's clothing out there, ready to sell you a dream but in reality their own dreams have amounted to zero. Watch out! I see you, silly rabbit! {giggle}

It was a gorgeous spring Saturday morning, sun blazing and I was dressed in a all-black T-shirt & skort, ready to face the "model calls" for the day. A "model call," is an audition if you will, where you present your headshot, comp card or model portfolio and deliver your walk to the fashion show producers and/or designers so they may decide whether "you're in or you're out" (in Heidi Klum's Project Runway voice).

Side-Bar: Some models choose not to do things in order and try to use their personality by smiling their way through. It's cute; however, they need to understand that while they are shining & smiling, the focus of the designers and judges have swayed over to someone else that showed up totally prepared. So it would behoove you to 1) make sure you fit the requirements before going to the call, 2) show up on-time, 3) dress appropriately, dress the part 4) bring the necessary tools for the call (i.e. shoes) in the same manner as if you were going to a corporate interview, and 5) put your game face on! In a nutshell, you need to go in "guns loaded".

These calls became the norm for any given weekend. They can be tedious due to the sometimes lengthy process and stressful due to the long waits, yet very fulfilling whenever you made the cut. There were times when I was chosen, and times where I was not.

As a matter of fact, this day was a callback from a model call. Chosen from 80 plus models, extremely excited because I wanted to walk for these talented nostalgic designers for a long time and it was for a major show. I showed up along with maybe 30 other models to present our walks; this time they did NOT want to see a couture walk, they wanted an urban strut which I've never done before. Watching the other ladies sachet back and forth, turning and turning, I'm like "well hell" not sure if I can do it quite like that but I'll try. Waiting in line, music loud, I heard a voice, "Did she say, next?" I asked the model next to me. She didn't know so I went ahead and placed myself in position and struck a pose.

    The choreographer asked for my name, twice, and gave me the nod to begin. As I lifted a foot to begin my walk, the choreographer jumped up, approached me and asked, "What's your name?" I stated my name, again. She then said, "Did I call you for the call back?" I said "yes." Then she loudly & abruptly said, "I don't know why, you are boring as hell" and proceeded to high-tale it to the middle of the room and yell at everyone else to get themselves together before they attempted to walk. Shocked and amazed to say the least. For a brief moment embarrassed. Other models apologized for her demeanor shrugging it off saying, "that's just how she is".

No ma'am it is NOT okay to overstep your authority because you profess to be celebrity, runway icon and a motivator. Just goes to show how you cannot judge a book by its cover, I respected her and she disappointed me. Now, I could've been just as rude and disrespectful as she; however I chose to be the better person and walk out the door after graciously thanking the designers for the experience with them. I was pissed to say the least but as you know everything that goes around comes back around.

It is not easy in the modeling industry and although I believe I have thick skin (so to speak) it is never easy experiencing rejection after putting your best foot forward. It comes with the territory but sometimes I gotta say OUCH! Rather than feel defeated it is times like this that encourage me and allow me to say "on to the next".

For months, I was having the time of my life, it seemed like I was in a show almost every other weekend. This one weekend was different, I was invited to help celebrate fashion designer Vanessa Henderson's birthday along with her then signature models. We danced, we laughed, and we posed as the shutters from the cameras snapped. A helluva fantastic time! Thinking I was one of the young "girls", not knowing my age, it was then Ms. Vanessa pinned me with the nickname of the "Barbie Doll" and thus becoming one of her signature models. Overtime, models became friends and friends became like sisters, we had a camaraderie. Likeminded people are a joy to my spirit and these ladies give me life!

For me the happenings for models were behind-the-scenes. I'm sure you would love to be a fly on the wall. Hair flying, shoes tossed, eyes rolling, tension flaring, words unspeakable and at the same time being pleasantly captured in a Behind-the-Scenes photo looking flawless. I think only models know how to fall into a "model pose" so easily without fail. After all the prep, comes the runway and hard work and preparations becomes life.

"When I model I pretty much go blank. You can't think too much or it doesn't work," as quoted by model, Paulina Porizkova. This is the place I go when I grace the runway. My idea place to be in my mind is sultry and sexy and to be seen in that moment at the top of the runway. After all, the goal of the runway is to not only sell the garment but to also be captured in photo for your portfolio. My image personifies confidence and sophistication and therefore my runway should mirror the same. There's nothing like being comfortable in my own skin and being free to be me.

Oh and let's not forget that a model must have photographs to be successful in the modeling industry. You cannot promote yourself as being a model without having done the work. As you change, your portfolio must change too.

I love being in front of the camera both filming and modeling; so much so that everyone in the family tends to split the room whenever I grab the camera because they know the next 30-45 minutes will be spent taking pictures of ME. The feeling of becoming one with the camera sends me to a happy place. If my sensory levels were involved I'd say my "happy" smelt like budding roses in a botanical garden, fresh-clean-new.

Nobody in my family loves the camera more than me but the one who owns the camera is my middle-child and daughter, Jenae Ann. My little tomboy didn't get the modeling bug until she was in high-school. She has studied all the super models, could tell you the names of all the top photographers, designers and stylist in the industry. Jenae Ann poses so effortlessly that the camera just embodies her every move. Camera & Jenae fit like a glove!

Photo 17 Ms. Jenae Ann Photo Shoot

In the meantime, she continues to coach "mom" and deliver tips from time-to-time. My latest tips for a photo shoot are to *smize* (smile with your eyes), be creative and show your personality, don't stay in a pose too long-keep moving, and if any anxiety-model through it. My daughter certainly knows her craft and with her continued persistence and vigor, her newly signed agency, she will meet her goal of being a Victoria Secrets and Sports Illustrated model in the near future.

Designer Gayla Rogers, has kept me busy for the past year not only with fashion shows but in being in front of the camera in her designs with photographers for various magazine shoots through which I made the cover of Luxe-Factor Magazine Nov. 2013. Connection upon connection I've managed to adjoin myself with professional caring people and I feel so blessed.

Like I said models are solicited for many different avenues of entertainment. One avenue I never considered for myself was that of a music video model. The call came and I was asked to be in a rap video. "Ladies I'm sitting this one out, how will I look being in a rap video? After all, my daughter was the lead model in the "Rack City remix" video. This would take following in her footsteps to another level, don't you think?" "DawnAngela stop tripping, it will be fun, it's a paid job and they are asking for mature models, so..." said my feisty friend. I agreed to be in the rap video with my model gal pals and we spent the better part of a Saturday evening onset as "eye-candy". A quick check mark alongside "music video model" and no need to revisit that again although fun experience.

    Let's not forget that the onset of me becoming a model everyone assumed I was between the ages of late 20s or early 30s. So for them I was just another one of the gals. For me it was a delight being among some of the best models realizing that I was succeeding doing what I wanted to do at this stage in my life and doing it well . . . sometimes better than the younger ladies. {giggle & wink}

Quotes to Keepin' it Movin':

"I believe that it's better to be looked over than it is to be overlooked." ~Mae West

"A girl should be two things Classy & Fabulous."
 ~Coco Chanel

"ZEST is the secret of all beauty. There is no beauty that is attractive without zest."
~Christian Dior

"An accessory is just as important as an outfit. It completes the look, highlighting the personality of the wearer."
~Giorgio Armani

MODEL CASTINGS:

There are two types of castings 1) for modeling jobs (Model Calls) and 2) for modeling agencies (Go-sees or Model Castings).

Model Calls: Modeling job castings are by clients that need models for various fashion shows, trade shows or print/magazine photo shoots. Typically, they will invite models that fit their requirements and have them appear in person so that the client can see who would be the best fit for the job. The models typically submit a comp card, headshot and/or bring their portfolio so that the client can see their work experience. If chosen, the client will officially book model and be paid for the job.

Go-Sees: Modeling agency casting calls are typically specific days and times during the week that anyone can come into the agency's office to be evaluated. If they are interested in you representing their agency you will be contacted at a later date to sign.

CHAPTER 9

Giving Back: VOLUNTEERISM

*"**Volunteerism**- the use or involvement of volunteer labor, esp. in community services"*

In today's society I think it necessary to give back to the community in whatever capacity may be fitting for you as an individual. It is our ministry.

As a young girl, on school holiday's I spent time with my mother at her place of employment, the Veteran's Administration. My mother worked for a psychiatrist. The dreary walk down the corridor seemed dark and scary; the sight of Mom's office door was welcome. Once beyond the walls and into mom's office I was okay and the visits were fun. Fun because I was able to entertain the patients that were in the ward. I fully didn't understand their sickness; however I could see that me being there singing and reading to them put a smile upon their face. I would also tag along with my parents to the nursing home visits which I felt extremely comfortable in serving the elderly. It soon became my job to push everyone around in their wheel chairs as we played music, sang and ministered to them. My "job" could've gone south the minute that I bumped a patient into a wall, but they allowed me to come back again and again.

A bit older, being that my father was a pastor I was introduced to the selfless act of giving as a ministry. Through established ministries at his church I often found myself with dad at various nursing homes, job core facilities, and serving the homeless. One of the outreach services he was proud to support were the missionaries in Haiti and the Philippines on a monthly basis. While it was perceived that our family had everything, we did not (we were comfortable), dad would give the shirt off his back, literally, if he needed to (and he did). It was instilled in me to "give" and whether it is material or brain knowledge I tried my best to assist those that were in need or perhaps needed a little encouragement.

Shared by Pastor Richardson (my dad):

"We can make a change if we practice the principles that Jesus taught . . . As the song by the late Marvin Gaye says, "Brother, Brother, there are so many of us crying. I was 40 years old before I went to college and if there is one thing that I won't allow young people to say around me its "I can't do it".

Personally, I feel it is extremely important to educate, and therefore, I made it a priority to support and volunteer my time to two non-profit organizations mostly catering to teens and women. Enchanted Closet, Inc. is a non-profit organization whose mission is to physically, mentally, and emotionally outfit Metro Atlanta high school girls from low-income families through programs that prepares them for social and professional milestones.

Serving on the solicitation committee of the foundations main Annual event, "Prom Dress Giveaway" started in 2003 as a project to provide prom dresses to teenage girls whose families were financially challenged. To-date Enchanted Closet has given away more than 5000 formal dresses to girls for prom is a joy to my heart. From all the leg work of preparation leading up to the day and then the actual day of being able to assist these girls from all different nationalities and all areas within Metro Atlanta was exhilarating to my soul.

Photo 18 Enchanted Closet participates in Nat'l Day of Service at MLK H.S., Atlanta, GA

Seeing the smiles on the faces of not only the girls but the mothers and fathers as well brought thoughts of "being Thankful". Know that these girls for the most part, left the event with full prom attire, from the dress to the accessories; they were fully loaded. For me, I was reminded of how important a gentle touch, a smile, a simple hello could mean to a person and definitely could have a lasting effect on a young girl/teen. I know for a fact and by experience that Prom time is stressful financially; therefore to offer a big prom dress boutique experience is more than phenomenal.

Recently, I have also been appointed as an Ambassador for Consciously Beautiful: I Am Enough a non-profit organization, whose mission is to empower women and girls to love the reflection that they see in the mirror. At the time of this writing I have not stepped into my position as Ambassador; however, my steps, my speech, my conversation with other women is one of positivity. It's an honor to represent because I truly feel that beauty comes from within and moves outwardly through self-confidence and the simple concept of feeling our best.

There's nothing more fulfilling than giving back. . . Giving-Giving-Giving is a gift, use it!

Photo 19 Consciously Beautiful: I Am Enough Ambassador photo

My Take Away from T.D. Jakes: Mind, Body and Soul:

- Volunteer, because even volunteering keeps you out there, exposed to different things.

Quotes to Keepin' it Movin':

"Give up self, Give up time, Give up emotion, to thrust upon another so they may heal."
~Dawn Angela Mickens

"Doing what you love is the cornerstone of having abundance in your life."
~ Wayne Dyer

"Don't wait around for other people to be happy for you. Any happiness you get you've got to make yourself."
~Alice Walker

DYING TO SELF

From the Desk of My Father, Rev. Robert Lee Richardson (1985)

When you are forgotten or neglected, or purposely set at naught, and you don't sting or hurt with the insult, or the over sight, but your heart is happy being counted worthy for Christ,
THAT IS DYING TO SELF.

When your good is evil spoken of, your wishes are crossed, your advice disregarded, your opinion ridiculed, and your refuse to let anger rise in your heart or even defend yourself, but take it all in patient loving silence,
THAT IS DYING TO SELF.

When you lovingly and patiently bear any disorder, any irregularity, any unpunctuality, or any annoyance when you stand face-to-face with waste, folly, extravagance, spiritual insensibility and endure it as Jesus endured it,
THAT IS DYING TO SELF.

When you are content with any food, any offering, any raiment, any climate, any society, any solitude, any interruption by the will of God,

THAT IS DYING TO SELF.

When you never care to refer to yourself in conversation or to record your own good works, or itch after commendation, when you truly love to be unknown,
THAT IS DYING TO SELF.

When you can see your brother prosper, and have his needs met, and can honestly rejoice with him in spirit and feel no envy, nor question God when your own needs are far greater and in desperate circumstances,
THAT IS DYING TO SELF.

When you can receive correction and reproof from one of less stature than yourself, and can humbly submit inwardly as well as outwardly, finding no rebellion or resentment rising up within your heart,
THAT IS DYING TO SELF.

ARE YOU DEAD YET?
In these days the spirit will bring us to the cross "That I may know Him…being made conformable to His death."

CHAPTER 10

Age is but a Number: MOTIVATION

*"**Motivation**: the act or process of giving someone a reason for doing something; the act or process of motivating someone"*

Have you ever been in a place when you just were NOT motivated? Have you ever been in such a funk that you didn't care about what in life was going on around you? Well, I know I have been in that place. So then, what do we do about it?

My thinking is to face the funk head on, to confront it with a vengeance and then work through it. It's actually easier than it sounds. No one knows your situation other than you and therefore it is solely your responsibility to get through the so-called funk. For example, I'm not going to lie; when I turned 40 it seemed like everything wanted to suddenly go wrong. I already wore glasses but my eyesight seemed to worsen from year-to-year. I'm a person who rarely ever gets sick yet I found myself with the occasional cold, a breast cancer scare, and I also had to have multiple polyps removed from my colon on two separate occasions. And then there was my figure; which suddenly had a mind of its own and decided to be flabby instead of fabulous. That was not going to work for me. I decided to turn my situation around by getting in sync with my physicians, drawing up a plan for corrective health, exercising and changing my mindset.

    I embraced the idea that beauty in and of itself is a mindset. That there is no defining age in when it comes to beauty; in other words age is but a number. I firmly believe that beauty comes from within and moves outwardly through self-confidence and the simple concept of feeling our best.

    I love being a woman! Being a woman is a wonderful thing. I believe that we as women carry our hearts on our shoulders and become the backbone and support of our families. Because so much is expected and required of us from others; we should desire much more of ourselves. You must first love the skin you're in and love the reflection that you see each day in the mirror. Once you are able to do that you will be more apt to love and appreciate the beauty of others.

Photo 20 DawnAngela

I am often asked how do I stay looking so young? I wish I could give a remedy, a concoction, or directions to the fountain of youth but I don't have any. My youthfulness is attributed to great genes first and then by surrounding myself with like-minded people with energy, stamina and drive. Other than that I try my best to drink water consistently throughout the day, eat healthy and exercise.

Photo 21 DawnAngela cover feature

Besides my mother; I am inspired by many women from all genres of fashion, film, and music. A few of the beauties over 40 that inspire me are Tina Turner, Diana Ross, Beverly Johnson, Angela Basset, Vivica Fox, and Cindy Crawford. All of these women have risen from humble beginnings to have successful careers in the fields in which we have grown to love them. They have also extended themselves beyond through philanthropy and/or creating thriving businesses of their own. Following the inspiration of these women is not only energizing but doubles as the confirmation for me to continue onward with my own destiny.

Photo 22 DawnAngela

What is it that keeps me motivated at the age 46? Well, first of all I am self-motivated in addition I thrive on positive feedback I receive from family and friends. At this pivotal point in my life, I have a strong desire to strive and achieve goals based on my own personal ambitions. I've always celebrated life and I have never had qualms when it comes to telling people my age. Being outspoken about it only changed when I entered into both the acting and modeling arenas. My ambition today is for people to recognize that there is a beautiful market for mature models as well.

Photo 23 DawnAngela

Recently I was asked to be a part of Ageless Beauty's roster of models and I am proud to have joined the crew. Ageless Beauty is a division of The Lyngale Agency in Atlanta where all of the models are aged 40 and beyond. It is quite impressive to see how the industry is slowly beginning to welcome the more mature women, as well as plus size women.

Now that my age is openly out there will things change for me? I don't believe it will. I am confident that the business is based on talent; therefore than everything should remain the same if not better.

Photo 24 Dawn Angela

My Take Away from T.D. Jakes: Mind, Body and Soul:

- Many people will tell you that it was not will power but Gods power that brought them through the storm.

Quotes to Keep it Movin':

"Age is but a number! Wear what you like and love what you wear! Forget your age!" ~ Kate Hudson

"The kind of beauty I want most is the hard-to-get kind that comes from within-strength, courage, dignity."
 ~Ruby Dee

CONCLUSION

Full Circle: Correlation with T.D. Jakes

As mentioned earlier, back in 2012 I made a video clip for BETs Network, T.D. Jakes Presents: Mind, Body & Soul. Since that time Season 1, Episode 10, 2013, the "Empowerment" segment has appeared several times of which a portion of my clip was shown. The episode also included special guest, Educator, Dr. Steve Perry. Again the episode was pertaining to those who found themselves unemployed and questioning their next move. Engulfed with anxiety as I taped the clip I realized that I was really in a deep place of uncertainty which sent me into a tail spin of rediscovery.

    The making of the video clip prompted me to "press the restart button" in my life and thus sending me on this glorious journey for the past 3 years. It was the airing of the Empowerment episode that sparked the emotion and inspiration to write this book.

Out of the blue I began to receive emails and/or Facebook inbox messages with job offers, words of encouragement and solutions to my "job situation." Really perplexed and annoyed from all the attention I just began to ignore the comments. You know what I mean? I marked most, as 'spam'! One day I received an email that read, "I received your information from Bishop Jakes' Mind, Body and Soul program. . ." STOP! "What did he say?" "He received my information from Bishop Jakes?" You know my head, cocked to the side, real quick and in a hurry. What was this guy talking about? Then it dawned on me that it was my video submission. Calls were received from family and friends both in and out-of-state inquiring if that was *me* on T.D. Jakes show. It was really crazy for a minute.

Side note: this was a year after I submitted the video clip so it wasn't clear to me at first that the correspondence had anything to do with my video clip. Wait a minute; I know BET wasn't giving away my information.

Hurriedly, I searched for the episode but couldn't find it-it had not yet been posted to BETs website. Weeks went by and I checked online again and again so I could see what all the hype was about. Then finally I viewed the episode and sure enough there I was looking as distraught and pitiful as ever. The clip was shortened so you really didn't hear my full statement which prompted me to go back and watch the full original submission clip.

My submission statement to T.D. Jakes Presents: Mind, Body & Soul:

"I've been unemployed for the past year and half after 20 years in the real estate industry. I want to know how I can stay motivated as a woman with a family. I feel like I'm not pulling my weight-I've worked all my life. I'm tired of being a homemaker and I'm so not a homemaker. How do I keep my head up?"

Upon watching the episode and subsequently re-watching my submission clip I became extremely emotional. Tears were streaming from my eyes uncontrollably. Happy tears I must say. It was in that moment that the Lord prompted me to pour my journey into a book.

I didn't quite understand it because I'm not a writer or a woman of patience. That evening I began writing into the wee hours of the next morning. Later that morning I felt free, released and excited as I embarked on a quest to expose my inner self to the world in the hopes of being an inspiration to other women who, like me, have found themselves unemployed, lost, or perhaps dissatisfied with themselves as they approach 40 years young and beyond—or who are just simply in a place of needing rejuvenation.

Photo 25 Dawn Angela

Being laid off turned into a blessing-in-disguise. I was granted the freedom to chase my lifelong dream. Current situation, in 2014, I am feeling immensely blessed at a fierce 46. I couldn't ask for a more richly fulfilled life. I am realizing my dreams at this stage in my life. However minimal they may seem to others, the fact of the matter is they are MY dreams being fulfilled. There is cause and effect each day of our lives and we have a choice to either be stagnant in our current state of mind or to learn to take chances and not take life so seriously. Life is too short. We are birthed into this world for a purpose so I encourage you to live YOUR purpose. Time stops for no one so whether you're 20, 30 or 40, just "keep it movin'."

Whew, writing is exhausting, who knew? To bring us full circle I will reply to those unanswered questions from the Introduction:

Who am I? Wife, mother, woman of faith, model, actress, philanthropist, motivator, author

What am I? Deserving, diligent, humble, giving, loyal, free spirit, witty, understanding, beautiful, intelligent

Where am I? A place of happiness, a place of peace, a place of calm, a place of accomplishment

In conclusion, life can be as hard and cruel as it can be wonderful. I don't know what tomorrow may bring; therefore, this is not the end of my story; it is just beginning, starting today.

"All great achievements require time."

~*Maya Angelou*

Like I said,

"Age is nothing but a Number"

#TimelessRebel

DawnAngela's Own Poems & Quotes

"Dare to be YOU! Dare to be TRUE! Dare to make the unbeliever a BELIEVER! It's all about YOU!"
~DawnAngela Mickens

***

Actions speak louder than word; words exasperate."
~DawnAngela Mickens

***

"If you don't get what you want; figure out a way to get it."
 ~DawnAngela Mickens

***

I can't be everything to everybody;
I can't be two places at the same time;
I can't extend myself further than I already have.
I can have Faith that God will provide my strength, my peace, my energy, my everything;
I can be a loving wife, I can be an understanding mom, I can be a confidant to a friend, and I can be complicated; however,
In being true to self, I can be who I am, ME!
~DawnAngela Mickens

***

It's not easy in the modeling industry and although I believe I have thick skin (so to speak). It's never easy experiencing rejection after putting your best foot forward. It comes with the territory but sometimes I gotta say OUCH! I'm still in it to win it SO, on to the next! :-)
~DawnAngela Mickens

***

LIVE SIMPLY, LOVE GENEROUSLY, CARE DEEPLY, SPEAK KINDLY.... LEAVE THE REST TO GOD
~DawnAngela Mickens

***

Life is like a roller coaster; you get jerked one way and another, and never know what's around the corner, but you just got to Enjoy the Ride!
~DawnAngela Mickens

Have you ever been hit with something so big that all you could do was say, Hmm?
I'm shutting it down and keeping it movin'...
~DawnAngela Mickens

***

Make a commitment to yourself to do the things you need to do to live a more enthusiastic life. I'm enthusiastic and I'm having fun!
~DawnAngela Mickens

***

Take a chance and stretch yourselves. Be embarrassed! Be hurt! Be scared! The rewards of growth and change are permanently rewarding!
~DawnAngela Mickens

***

Be inspired, Be challenged, Be real, Be yourself, and Be open, so you too can experience that freeing moment that allows you to say "Hello, ME, I Love You & I Am Enough"!
~DawnAngela Mickens

MODEL RESUME (highlights)

RUNWAY

2014

Beach Bling Swimwear: Spring & Summer Heat Show

Urban vs. Couture Designer Competition, designer Gayla Rogers

4th Annual Legendary Awards Fashion Show "Glitz, Glam & Style Runway"

Hype Magazine Meet & Greet

"Embracing the Philippines" designer Gayla Rogers

Couture for Change: Into the Wild Designer Completion

2013

The Fashion Event ATL designer CoutureCouture Brigitte Marie

5th Annual RAWards Indie Arts Awards" designer Gayla Rogers

"Couture-Couture" SBC Extravaganza Jewelry designer Ancient Future and Beyond by Baba G

"Queens of the Night" designer Linda Bezuidenhout Apparel

LABELAtlanta 2013 "Tribute to CFDA Fashion Legend Designer Stephen Burrows" designer, Vanessa Henderson, The House of Van Miller

Couture Fashion Elements: "Fresh off the Runway"

Beach Bling: "Summer Heat"

Dwight Eubanks "Legends of Fashion"

2012
Fashionista Next Door (The Gap)

"Celebrating the Man behind the Mask"

Diva Day International "Goodies Couture"

Dwight Eubanks "Beauty & Glamour"

F.a.B.; Fashion against Bullying

PRINT
Chy'Ann Magazine- March 2014	Feature
ModelCall Magazine-Jan/Feb 2014	Feature
Luxe-Factor Magazine -Nov 2013	Cover
Luxe-Factor Magazine-Sept 2013	Feature
Urban Mainstream Magazine-Issue 60/2011	Feature

STOCK PORTFOLIO
Essence Online Magazine- June 2014

PROMOTIONAL
Exclusiv Vodka/NBRPA Celebrity Mixer
VIP Hostess

Republic of Couture Grand Opening
VIP Hostess

Sprint Promotional Networking Event
VIP Hostess

Espada Tequila Launch Event
Brand Ambassador

HIGHLIGHTS OF ACTING/BACKGROUND RESUME

FILM
The Good Lie					Airplane Passenger

Last Vegas					Party Girl

Hunger Games: Catching Fire
						District 11

Scary Movie 5   Ballet Attendee

Devil's Knot   Featured/Reporter

Madea's Witness Protection
                             Church Attendee

Flight   Featured/NTSB

What to Expect When You're Expecting
                             Featured/Pregnant
                             Convention Lady

TELEVISION

The Rickey Smiley Show-Season 2
                             Church Congregation

The Watson's Go to Birmingham
                             Church Congregation

The Have and The Have Nots
                             Birthday Party Guest

In The Meantime   Pedestrian

Second Generation Wayans-Season 1
          Stand-In for Faune Chambers

Let the Church Say Amen
          Featured/Matron-of-Honor

Vampire Diaries-Season 4
          Featured/T. Sousa

Raising Izzie   Church Attendee

Necessary Roughness-Season 2
          Featured/Courtroom Clerk

For Better or Worse-Season 2
          Salon Patron

Single Ladies-Season 2
          Boutique Patron

The Following-TV Pilot   FBI Agent

Let's Stay Together-Season 2   Lounge Patron

House of Payne-Season 7   Courtroom Attendee

COMMERCIAL

Budweiser (6/2013)	Football Patron
Emory Healthcare Commercial (6/2013)	Patient
Belk	Belk Charity Day Sale
La Nonna's Italian Restaurant	Restaurant Patron
KFC	Mom

UP NEXT

Currently cast and filming in Atlanta
"I Do Maybe, The Movie", release 2015

RESOURCES

Chapter 6
Harris, Elena. SpiritAnimal.com Editor "Butterfly Spirit Animal & Totem"
http://www.spiritanimal.info/butterfly-spirit-animal/

Chapter 8
Crawford, Cindy. "Advice to Aspiring Models"
http://www.cindy.com/about-me 2012

Chapter 10
Unknown. "Southside's Formula: Diversity: Rev. Robert Richardson Leads Church On the Move." The Observer Newspaper 7-13 Feb. 1985. Print.

ACKNOWLEDGEMENTS

With thanks and special gratitude to:

Shekina Moore of Literacy Moguls, who believed in me and guided me through the process of becoming a first time published author.

Anthony Page of Blue Bistro Creative for the fabulous layout of the front & back covers of the book.

Susan Dilworth of Dilworth PR, my lovely, business savvy PR agent who is branding and guiding me to becoming the business woman I intend to be. www.dilworthpr.com

Mad Scientist Productions (Carl) for taking my descriptive imagery and creating an awesome logo and business cards.

BET Networks, T.D. Jakes: Mind, Body and Soul (S1/Ep. 10 "Empowerment") for unknowingly provoking energy and light into my soul; thus giving me the inspiration to write this book.

With a humble "Thank You" to:
    Ardre Orie, Author of Consciously Beautiful: I Am Enough for seeing my inner self and welcoming me into the fold as an Ambassador.

    Bonita Johnson, President and CEO of Enchanted Closet for allowing me to channel my energies as a volunteer and supporting my acting gigs by way of dresses from the Enchanted Closet Boutique gown.

With my undying "koodles" to:
    Ms. Nickee Mack of Diva Day International, Inc. for accepting me into the agency and successfully groom into the fine model that I am today. www.divadayinternational.com

    Tina Bridges of Ageless Beauty/Lyngale Agency for seeing my sophistication, taking an interest and welcoming me to the agency.

For friendship and sisterhood to the Models:
    Katrina Walker, Terrasea Page, Keri Steward, Anashay Gould, Shana Green; my sisters that have been with me every step of the way, Love you to pieces, you give me Life!

To my designers (my friend/my mentor) for creating fabulous designs that make me feel comfortable in my skin:

    Gayla Rogers, Gayla Rogers Collections (GRC), and Vanessa Henderson, the House of Van Miller.

To my photographers, who never skip a beat and make sure to capture my best "shot":

    Jamie Thomson/702 Photo Studio, Charlton Hudnell/MyMiracleMoments Photography, John Washington, Jr./JWJ Photography, Cedric Pitts/BlackTie Photography, and Tim Rogers/TWR Photography

For their belief, strength and unconditional love to:

    Jaeda Lee Mickens, Jenae Ann Mickens, Darryl Joshua Mickens, Rachaelle Lynne Richardson, Tanisha Jacobs, Dorothy Ann Richardson and my doggie, Polo Mickens

To my biggest supporter, my husband, Darryl, who has supported, provided, guided, and loved me through the long days and agonizing long nights of this journey thus making sure that my dreams come true. Thank you and I Love You!

www.ingramcontent.com/pod-product-compliance
Lightning Source LLC
Chambersburg PA
CBHW070456100426
42743CB00010B/1641